W9-DGN-121

lemur

Please visit our web site at: www.garethstevens.com
For a free color catalog describing Gareth Stevens' list of high-quality books
and multimedia programs, call 1-800-542-2595 (USA) or 1-800-461-9120 (Canada).
Gareth Stevens Publishing's Fax: (414) 332-3567.

Library of Congress Cataloging-in-Publication Data

Johnson, Jinny.
    Lemur / by Jinny Johnson; [illustrated by Ch'en-Ling; photography by Susanna Price].
  —North American ed.
       p. cm. — (Busy baby animals)
    ISBN 0-8368-2926-3 (lib. bdg.)
     1. Ring-tailed lemur—Infancy—Juvenile literature. [1. Ring-tailed lemur. 2. Lemurs.
  3. Animals—Infancy.] I. Ch'en-Ling, ill. II. Price, Susanna, ill. III. Title.
  QL737.P95J64   2001
  599.8'3—dc21   2001020529

This North American edition first published in 2001 by
Gareth Stevens Publishing
A World Almanac Education Group Company
330 West Olive Street, Suite 100
Milwaukee, Wisconsin 53212 USA

This U.S. edition © 2001 by Gareth Stevens, Inc. Original edition © 2000 by
Marshall Editions Developments Ltd. First published by Marshall Publishing Ltd.,
London, England.

Illustrations: Ch'en-Ling
Photography: Susanna Price
Editor: Elise See Tai
Designer: Caroline Sangster
Gareth Stevens editor: Katherine J. Meitner
Gareth Stevens cover design: Katherine A. Kroll

Printed in the United States of America

1 2 3 4 5 6 7 8 9 05 04 03 02 01

lemur

Jinny Johnson

Gareth Stevens Publishing
A WORLD ALMANAC EDUCATION GROUP COMPANY

Beza was born
tiny and helpless.
Now she is bigger
and can explore
all by herself.

Beza is ready to try new foods. Her mother shows her yummy fruits to eat.

Which fruits should she try first?

Beza has a big family of twenty lemurs. When she is afraid, she cries out, and someone in the family comes to help.

Lemurs love to climb and leap. Beza's claws help her hold on to branches.

Look at Beza's striped tail. It is longer than her body! Lemurs hold their tails up to "talk" to other lemurs.

When Beza is tired, her mother carries her up into a tree for the night. They snuggle there with the rest of the family. Sleep tight, Beza.

More about Lemurs

Ring-tailed lemurs live in woodlands and forests on the island of Madagascar. They are primates, just like their monkey and ape relatives. Although they are good climbers, lemurs spend most of the day on the ground, looking for fruit, leaves, and flowers to eat. They sleep in trees and like to sunbathe on branches. Female lemurs stay with the group, or troop, in which they were born. Male lemurs leave their families when they become adults. They wander with other males or find a new troop to join.